Listen!

Other Books by Peter Brook Published by TCG

Conversations with Peter Brook
(edited by Margaret Croyden)

Evoking (and forgetting!) Shakespeare

The Prisoner
(with Marie-Hélène Estienne)

The Quality of Mercy: Reflections on Shakespeare

The Shifting Point: Theatre, Film, Opera 1946-1987

Peter Brook

PLAYING BY EAR

Reflections on Sound
and Music

THEATRE COMMUNICATIONS GROUP

NEW YORK

2020

Playing by Ear is copyright © 2019 by Peter Brook

Playing by Ear is published by Theatre Communications Group, Inc.
520 Eighth Avenue, 24th Floor, New York, NY 10018-4156

This volume is published in arrangement with Nick Hern Books
Limited, The Glasshouse, 49a Goldhawk Road, London W12 8QP

Lines from 'Sea Fever' by John Mansfield quoted with kind permission
of The Society of Authors as the Literary Representative of the Estate
of John Mansfield.

This publication is made possible in part by the New York State
Council on the Arts with the support of Governor Andrew Cuomo
and the New York State Legislature.

TCG books are exclusively distributed to the book trade by
Consortium Book Sales and Distribution.

A catalogue record for this book is available from the Library of Congress.

ISBN 978-1-55936-983-1 (paperback)

Front cover image © Fer Gregory/Shutterstock.com
Author photo by Régis d'Audeville

First TCG Edition, June 2020

Contents

Part Two

Acknowledgements

For three out of the countless fine people to whom I am eternally grateful. Three are very close as I write:

Olivier Mantei, not only for his close friendship over so many years, but also for the special sensitivity he brings to every question, nourished by his life in music. But above all for his encouragement to write this book after I had spoken about music in a radio show he had asked me to do.

To Franck Krawczyk, as the inseparable partner in so many explorations.

And equally to Toshi Tsuchitori, who embodies listening with his eyes, his mind and his body until they emerge from the tips of his fingers. Whatever the style—ancient, traditional, Eastern, Western, classical or jazz—they are reborn every moment he plays.

And once again, for reasons I have already expressed in previous books—Nina.

'The past is history, the future is mystery—the present is a gift, that's why it's called the present.'

Words I heard recited by a bus driver to his passengers at the end of a long day. Where he got it from I didn't ask and will never know, but it has stayed with me over at least fifty years.

Astrology today is a despised science, yet we have come to realise that at the moment of birth we carry within us what is now called a genetic structure, which conditions our tastes, our prejudices, our compassion, our hatreds, our intuition. All of these thread their way through our life as we head towards a destination which we cannot know but which the stars and our genes lead us to—that point where the many threads intertwine, making a pattern that only appears when the last page is turned.

Prologue

'Do you like music?' The question is as absurd as saying, 'Do you like food?' There is food that is tasteless, indigestible, sits heavily on the organs, but there is the vast range of foods that can give relief, nourishment, often pleasure. As Orpheus discovered, every animal can respond to sounds. For us, the living question is 'Which sounds? What music?' In this book we will try to explore together the infinite range of experiences that can sometimes touch us deeply, sometimes leave us cold.

PART ONE

The Birth of Form

The very first tremor in the eternal nothingness was a sound, a sound which can only be recognised once the human organism has evolved a capacity to respond—in other words, once there is a listener. In the process of creation, with sound came the presence of time—time that measures everything for us humans from dawn to dusk, from here to eternity.

The very first sounds from which gradually music was born inevitably had a sequence, an unwinding thread, that eventually leads to the sense of long, long phrases. And here, whatever the context, but above all in the performing arts, we touch on the essential. The long phrase is composed of an infinite number of details, a music where the beauty lies in the heart of each fragment, because it fills and reaches out of one unique space. This leads us to the recognition that every human attempt to determine what fills the space is a poor, a very poor reflection of the detail that is placed and brought to life by a source way beyond the wishes, the inventiveness and the ambitions of the individual. For this reason I deplore any of us, young or old, being called creators. Creation has only one source far beyond our understanding. This is where the form is born from the formless. *Our* role, like that of a good gardener, is respectfully to recognise that only when the ground has been lovingly prepared, can the true form be ready to receive the nourishment with which it can grow, develop and open.

There have been countless tales of how the world began, countless attempts to cope with the mystery of creation.

In Africa, where every tribe has its own creation tale, there are those that speak of a fine rope coming from the sky, down which the first man slid to Earth. Or else of the Earth opening for a man to clamber out.

But a very special tale comes from a tiny obscure tribe. Here, it is emptiness that is evoked, a vast nothingness. Then out of a timeless nothing comes a vibration, a sound, and from this original sound comes every aspect of creation. This tale blends at once with 'the Word'—the source of all the forms humanity learnt to know.

In the rich heyday of the sixties, from New York to San Francisco, from the East to the West Coast, young America was vibrating with the need to throw away all known forms and ideas in the wild search for something new. As always when Pandora's Box is opened, a confusing mixture tumbles out. There was Andy Warhol, there was Julian Beck with the Living

Theatre, there was Joe Chaikin with his Open Theater, and there was the cult of drugs, from LSD to marijuana, in which the miraculous universe, until then hidden in every detail, could now be felt and lived. I remember at six o'clock one morning seeing in a coffee shop a man who had spent the whole night smoking pot. He had ordered a waffle, and as I came in he was deeply concentrated on filling each dent in the waffle's surface with maple syrup, lovingly watching the passage of every drop. 'This is the most beautiful task I have ever given myself. It's worth living for.'

And as I myself plunged into this vibrant world of painters, actors and musicians, I was told of a composer in New York whom I had to meet. I was taken to his apartment in the Village. He warmly led me to where his wife was sitting, holding a cello. He took up a violin and played a single note. She listened attentively and joined him with the same note from her cello. She sustained the sound after his sound had ended, and when she could sustain her own no longer there was no pause, he picked up the same note. And so it continued. There was no end. It became unendurable. I began to fidget, then to speak, asking for some word of explanation. Politely, they put down their instruments. 'Our aim,' she said, 'is to make more and more people pick up this sound. Gradually, it can spread. It can cross the land, go from continent to continent, until one day it can link more and more human beings until we are all united. It can become the World Sound. We've done a recording. Would you like to hear it?' I got up and fled.

The aim of linking the world with a single sound was a natural part of the romantic enthusiasm of the time, but the essential quality of life was very easily forgotten. Life can never repeat itself. Every moment carries within it the possibility of new creation.

My First Teacher

'Don't sway. Don't beat time with your body. You're not a dancer. Just sit up straight, don't move, just listen.'

She was a friend of my mother's, and, like her, from Russia. She had studied the piano in Moscow and, now living in London, gave lessons. I was just twelve and had already had some boring lessons from impatient ladies. Her real name was Vera Vinagradova, but we called her simply Mrs Biek. Right away she put a Mozart sonata in front of me: luckily it was called 'Sonata Facile'. 'Try to read the notes.' At once, the challenge. With the sound of the first note, a call for quality. 'As your fingers touch the note, listen to the sound your fingers have made and don't allow any tensions in the shoulders, the arms, the fingers. You've done your job. Just let it flow. And be ready for the next note, press, let go, listen.' And very, very soon she would add, 'When you've learnt the first movement, you must play it to someone else, to your mother, your brother. The only reason for you to learn music is not for yourself. It's to share it with others.'

Very soon, I discovered that this went very far. Every couple of months she would rent a room in the Wigmore Hall. All the families were invited and the pupils would be called on to play, as best they could. This brought purpose and meaning to the classes, and the progress was often astonishing. I remember a fat, middle-aged Russian who, like many émigrés in wartime, was making his living on the black market. As a child, he hadn't had music lessons, and the regret over the years had never left him. Meeting Mrs Biek he at once put himself in her hands. A few months later, at one of her concerts, he was playing an intricate piece of Franz Liszt.

The true challenge came in my first year at Oxford. Mrs Biek had given me a Mozart concerto to play with her on two pianos. I came down from Oxford for the concert and was terrified. In those days, it was fashionable for students, especially before exams, to take sniffs of Benzedrine. I did so resolutely, in the train and in the dressing room, waiting for my turn to come. Little did I know the other side of Benzedrine. When I sat down at the keyboard my hands were trembling. I could see they were going to be on the next note or the one before it. But the necessity not to betray my teacher and spoil the evening somehow calmed me down, and all went well.

Parents are always encouraging their children to show off to their friends. Perhaps it's a piece on the family piano, perhaps a song or some steps of dance. Or even surprising acrobatics. There is always a reward: a hug, a kiss or a 'Bravo!' Always a reward, soothing for a moment the sense of inadequacy that is always there. If gradually one skill grows more than another, inevitably the answer to the eternal question 'What do you want to do when you grow up?' is nurtured. Waiting in the wings, ready to leap, are Success and Ambition. Then, as I became caught up in the world of art, I realised how deeply hidden is this need to get the approval of others and how many forms it can take.

Applause is the most obvious expression of approval. With applause comes relief and reassurance. I have seen opera singers in the wings counting the number of times the soloists are called back. 'Oh, she's not much good. She only got two calls.'

Of course, there is also plenty of love and joy in the exploration of what becomes one's special field. For each of us, this 'field' comes with its own possibilities and limitations. To each of us is given this or that talent—to one, cooking; to another, maternity. A performer can only succeed if the field is truly his or her own. I am often asked by parents what is the best way to help children who are convinced they want to be actors. 'Put every possible obstacle in their way.' It is only those whom nothing can stop that can cross all the barriers of frustration, disappointment and above all waiting for a call that may never come. I was once looking for an actor with a very special physique—a round face and a massively round body. After many false attempts I came across a photo in a casting directory that corresponded exactly to what was needed. There was a phone number, and, although it was Sunday, I called at once. For a long time there was no answer and when in the end a timid voice came on the line, I made our proposal. 'Wow! I was putting the joint in the oven and I said to myself, 'I've been waiting for that bloody phone to ring for far too long.' If the phone doesn't ring before I take the joint out I will give up acting for good.'

A performer is a human being and has hundreds of known and unknown levels of insecurity. Looking at the tough, competitive world around us, we are inevitably full of doubts about our own ability to succeed, comparing our own talents with those around us. Fame expresses itself not only in offers but also in the fees that are offered. 'Is he/she bankable?' A phrase we often hear.

The soloist is the one whose identification with his or her name—their label—is the most apparent. Many covet prizes, and praise in all the media. But the real talent carries a purity within it. The best actors I have known, like John Gielgud and Paul Scofield, had a fine sensibility that dissolves the barriers of inevitable ego.

Tradition

Dead or Alive
Lethal or Life-giving

No one can breathe life into old bones. Hanging on to the past easily brings sclerosis—the past is past. But traditions, if relived in the present, can be a vital force, bringing new life to old forms. Then, as the old forms reveal their riches and their splendour, so in the very special area of music, thanks to the support of the past, new life can come to us.

The sad situation is that pupils cannot find their way alone. But as their music ceases to be a vocation and becomes a profession, their teacher has to relay and transmit the known existing forms. There is only the very rare exception to this rule: in Paris all her pupils express their adoration and gratitude to Nadia Boulanger. For us to feel and understand her specialness we can read one of the pieces she wrote called—revealingly—'On Attention', where we can feel how she has sensitively liberated herself from being stuck to the surface, however beguiling the surface may seem. Every fine musician—soloist or conductor—that I have had the joy of knowing would always say after a performance that went specially well: 'Tonight, I could feel it was not me, it was the music that played through me.' This calls for a fine sensitivity in the player, which in turn awakes the same quality in the listener.

We must always be aware of false teaching—Western music is dominated so often by the metronome and the tyranny of the conductor shouting 'Follow the beat.' The fine interpreters, from Glenn Gould to Claudio Abbado, are always floating and skimming freely across pitch and rhythm, which are there as a scaffolding to be respected but never allowed to dominate. In so much of Asian music, especially Indian, its quality demands constantly to be renewed.

We are called on to be vigilant, to beware how quickly the seed of death can replace the flow of life and a living tradition can become arthritic, rigid, lifeless. Like an embalmed corpse—such as the one on Red Square—it can be venerated as if there was still life in Lenin's body.

Our greatest guide we carry within ourselves: our sense of boredom. We can immediately recognise a deadly bore by the way they tirelessly repeat their ideas and stories using more and more words. Boredom is our secret signal that what once was, is now no longer. But like everything, the consequences have two sides to them. In music, in theatre, indulging the temptation to seize the latest tricks is not enough to renew a life that has been lost.

There is one process both in England and in France—even in Russia—that chokes off everything that can bring new life to music and drama. That process is 'repetition'. In French, one word—*répétition*—contains in itself the worst of dangers, as though there is a virtue, day after day, in repeating. In English, the word is far worse. It is 'rehearsal'. When we call for a rehearsal, do we ever pause to listen to this awesome word? Crouched in the middle, between the 're' and the 'l', is the hearse, the wagon that carries the lifeless body to the grave. 'Deadly' is a warning: it can be opposed; all hope is not yet lost. But the hearse carries the box to finality. It is the end product of 'repeating'. A commonly accepted notion handed down by tradition comes to us through teachers.

Every so-called rehearsal, every practising, allows the dark detail to grow. For this, we need more and more to discover what helps in this process, what stands in its path. This came to me in an unexpectedly simple way.

At the end of the war, there was a Belgian pianist who had moved to London. One day I visited him before a concert. He was practising, sitting at the keyboard with no music in front of him, only a carefully opened copy of the *Evening News*, which he was reading contentedly. His daughter was sitting beside him, the score open on her lap. If at any moment her dad made a mistake, she would correct him. I saw at once that the saying I had grown up with—'Practice makes perfect'—was quite untrue. Practice is raking and watering the soil; the burgeoning will only appear if we hear in ourselves another phrase that carries all we need to know—'Pay attention!' In the case of my concert pianist friend, all his attention was taken up with the day's news, hence the mistakes. But true attention is what enables the acrobat spinning into space unerringly to place his foot on that tiny patch of security offered by the hand or shoulder of his partner.

The life of a form cannot be imposed. Conductors, performers who repeat what worked the day before are already carrying in their action the kiss of death. The choice is between the deadly or the living.

Field of Battles

He never came to these sessions, which were the orchestra's own exercise.

They began once more and suddenly everything changed: the life of the music was there, miraculously by itself. Joyfully they relaxed, and the music lived between them. Then one of the players, at a moment when his instrument had a pause, raised his head. He saw that at the back of the top circle their conductor had quietly slipped in. He stood motionless, listening, and the pure quality of his listening filled the space, informing and inspiring the orchestra. The day was saved.

In staging too, actors within a living ensemble can allow their exchanges with their partners, their entrances and their exits, their gestures to be both uniquely their own and yet still serve the rhythms and the melodies of the unbroken line.

This is even more true in music. A sonata is a whole, a symphony is a whole. If any detail is blurred, the meaning of the phrase is lost. But the temptation to be in love with one's own sound too easily comes at the expense of line. For this reason, teachers who count, who use the metronome, are destroying the true flow. There are pauses, there are intervals; a symphony has four parts, and the passage from one movement to another can cross the change of mood through silence. Most concertgoers have long since learnt never to applaud between movements. Claudio Abbado went further when he said that a moment of silence at the end of a work before the inevitable explosion of applause was for him the only way of knowing that the embodiment of the music had been true. This is the limitation of virtuosity in the often dazzling brilliance of execution: the infinitesimal detail loses its uniqueness. The nearest metaphor I can find is breathing. Whether in speed or in slowness there must always be the space for the work to breathe, and only then can its essential life appear.

In the same way, in a true realisation of an opera, there is such harmony between the conductor, orchestra, soloists and choruses in all their movements across the stage that there emerges an ever-renewed sense of detail and flow, of form not as an architecture but as a current. A five-act opera is one long phrase. For Wagnerians this is the magic of Wagner. For Schumann, Schubert's last symphony had '*eine himmlische Länge*', a heavenly length.

If there are six words that have swept across the world and are recognised everywhere out of all context, they are 'To be or not to be'. In music, in the same way, there is an instant recognition of the three notes and the chord, twice repeated, that introduce Beethoven's Fifth Symphony. These are often presented as an imperative call for attention, but there was one time when they took on a different meaning. This was at Aix, when the very talented and very young conductor Daniel Harding opened a concert with Beethoven's Fifth. I have never heard it attacked at such an almost unbelievable speed. This was the tempo the young Toscanini had brought to Mozart's Symphony in G minor. In both cases we were blown out of our preconceptions—and almost out of our seats.

Fat Paunches

The director of the Staatsoper—the principal opera house in Berlin—took me on my first visit to see all the many parts of his theatre during a performance. We saw the workshops, the wardrobes, the dressing rooms, the scene docks. Then he opened a small door and led me up many steps to the top gallery. It was the middle of *Der Rosenkavalier*. Looking down, I saw the audience in the front rows of the stalls. The seats were naturally the most expensive, and everyone in them recognised that a night at the opera demanded their most carefully chosen and most elegant clothes. The women wore *haute couture* while their husbands were in black—and even white—tie. Of all operas, *Rosenkavalier* was a specially loved object. They would tell envious friends that they had tickets for the first night and would hum the famous waltz as they dressed. What I saw, looking down from the gods, were rows and rows of portly gentlemen, fast asleep. I understood that for the wealthy, opera was not only a sleeping draught but also a valuable preparation for cultivated conversations at the dinner parties that would follow.

For New York, Tchaikovsky was a star name: at concerts, at the ballet, there was always an enthusiastic, devoted audience—a joy for impresarios, as there was no risk: the house would always be full. I was asked to direct *Eugene Onegin* at the Metropolitan Opera House. Its new director, Rudolf Bing, after a successful career in Germany, had created the Edinburgh Festival. It seemed an obvious choice for New York to appoint him to take charge of the Met. Little did either of us imagine that there could be any risk in opening the season with *Onegin*.

I loved the work, from the first simple, touching phrases of the introduction through to the final duel—all reflecting the impeccable marriage between the music and Pushkin's story and characters. A true marvel, a sensitive and dynamic Greek conductor, Dimitri Mitropoulos, and a beautifully hand-picked cast—as only the Met could afford—made this a thrilling adventure. I would meet up with Bing to discuss the day's work and—unique in my experience of opera-house directors—he would apologise deeply for the unfair pressure the director had to endure from the inflexible and intertwining rules of a series of unions—unions for the musicians, for the stage crew, for the soloists, for the chorists—often in complete contradiction with one another, calling for breaks just at the moment that a certain life and freedom was entering the rehearsal. Bing could do nothing, though he vowed to fight this situation in the coming years, fully aware of how detrimental it was to the quality of the production. Furthermore, having shared with me the problems of the lack of continuity caused by the inevitable dropping of the curtain at the end of every scene as the stagehands changed the scenery, he proposed that Mitropoulos should write little interludes, using only the material of the score, so as to sustain the flow. I was delighted: the interludes grew out of the score as though they had been composed from the start by Tchaikovsky himself.

So where did we go so wrong? What was the hidden pitfall just waiting for us? Neither of us had realised that the Opening Night of the Season at the Met was, for New Yorkers, a tremendous social event. Editors had already prepared pages in *The New York Times*, the *Wall Street Journal* and the other voices of the town, while one newspaper, *Women's Wear Daily*, was only interested in how the females were dressed—and by whom: their jewels, their hairstyles, their hats, their shoes. The only reason to be present at the Opening Night was to be seen, photographed, admired and then ecstatically approved—or bitchily commented on—by the other members of a self-loving section of society, the Jet Set. All of this could have been harmless—as it had been over years with works of real quality by Verdi, Puccini, and Gounod. Why was Tchaikovsky not allowed to fall into place with the others?

One simple reason. In every performance of the known repertoire the great demanding moments were the major arias. The joy of the first night as much for the tiara'd beauties in the boxes as for the enthusiastic members of the upper circle and the gallery—also as well dressed as possible for the occasion—was the possibility again and again throughout the evening to plunge into baths of bravos and applause as preparation for the ultimate explosion at the end as each soloist took his calls.

None of us had noticed that Tchaikovsky had not written an Italian-style finale to the arias. He wished the story to flow on, so the audience raised their white-gloved hands only to find that the final chord had discreetly passed them by. Even worse, the end of each scene had its applause frustrated by Mitropoulos's musical links. Time and again the audience blamed the composer, Tchaikovsky, and then the Intendant, Rudolf Bing. How absurd! What a miserable choice for a great occasion for which we were all so well prepared.

The next day, even Tchaikovsky got a lukewarm press.

When at Covent Garden I could choose my own opera to work on, I chose *Salome*, as there was an extraordinary and powerful singer ready to take every risk in the title role: Ljuba Welitsch. I had no problem with Strauss's dense and elaborate score, as it seemed the perfect expression of Oscar Wilde's highly colourful writing. But I wanted to make a stage image that could be worthy of the score. So I asked Salvador Dalí to design the setting and the costumes . . . but that is another story, which I have written about in detail in my book *Threads of Time*.

Herbert von Karajan was a superb showman. He invented many tricks. At a performance of Verdi's *Otello* at the Vienna Opera, when the house lights went down, the audience eagerly awaited the star conductor's arrival—hands and voices ready for a loud fanfare of applause. The orchestra was already tuned, all eyes were on the left of the pit, where the conductor would enter. A long, long pause. Nothing happened. When the wait had become almost unendurable, suddenly from the opposite side of the pit Karajan came running on. His leap onto the podium was the upbeat for the orchestra, and so, as his feet landed, the curtain rose, and with the thundering notes of the orchestra, the audience was swept into an image of whirling clouds and choristers looking for shelter from the coming storm. An unforgettable beginning!

Similarly, in a very different context, I was fortunate enough to be present at Toscanini's farewell concert in New York. This conductor had brought to symphonic music a vitality, a dynamic tempo, a force that drove the work to its conclusion with such breathtaking verve that no listener could avoid being swept away, even for a moment, by the current. Visually, this expressed itself in the vigour of the conductor, in the whole of his body, and in the range of gestures that became a spellbinding dance to inspire orchestra and audience, all in the same breath. And so the well-dressed American audience had come to the maestro's last performance, convinced that it would be the greatest of firework displays.

A fine old man came onto the podium: one small gesture—and the band began to play. From then on, Toscanini hardly moved at all. No gestures, just listening with tiny movements of the head as his attention settled on one of the groups of instruments. He had played so often with this orchestra and had rehearsed every detail so many times that it was simply the quality of his listening which could call from the attentive and loving players the finest of music, surpassing the greatest moments even in Toscanini's career.

A Long Phrase

'A play of Shakespeare is one long phrase.' This is the best indication one can give to actors and directors. There is an invisible line that passes through the astonishing richness of movements, rising high, then falling low, in the words, the characters, the relationships. Ideally, this demands a sense of continuity, of flow, like a stream passing over rocks, boulders, waterfalls, but always flowing to the sea.

Hit or Miss

There is a very simple way—using, thank God, no words or definitions—to evoke true listening. Look at a cat. It hears and responds to the slightest sound with a listening that involves every cell in the body. It may be 'pss, pss!', 'tt, tt, tt', or just the clink of its dish being placed on the kitchen floor. There is no time for thought. The question, the alertness, is at once in every part of the body. This goes for every feline creature: tigers, panthers, leopards—all the same.

With other animals, there is a similar alertness in the head and in the neck, but with a horse, for example, the body down to the legs is totally given to the dynamic needs of its muscles to execute what the sound demands. In the cat, the question 'What?' evoked by the tiniest sound is an instant response that embodies wonder.

There is listening and listening, depending on the degree of interest. A cat's interest, its readiness, is always there. What is the simple link between the motionless readiness and the instantaneous response? This leads us to a word no dictionary can explain. Being 'touched'. Everyone knows from direct experience what this means. 'I am touched, deeply touched by . . . !' When we say a pianist has a good touch, we do not mean a technique that could be learnt in a conservatoire. We mean fingers that, like a cat, are so alert to the vibrations that it gives life to the finger.

We have deep down in us a level where all rhythms are instantly recognised—there is no need for effort. This is clear in all forms of verse, rhyming or otherwise. An actor does not need to strive to reach the form of blank verse—or in French of alexandrines. They were already there for the writer, who was guided all the time by this inaudible beat. The simplest way to see this is to think of the limerick—the form, the structure, the sequence of rhymes is in us since childhood. We have only to hear one word like 'Jack' and, if we are in a limerick mood, we will immediately complete the line: 'There once was a fellow called Jack'. And then all the rhymes—sack, rack, pack, back, tack, lack, etc.—fly into our mind for us to choose.

This is the process out of which unique sonnets and sublime sonatas can arise, almost—though not completely—as though by themselves. We have to be there, ready, attentive, with a sensitivity highly honed, or else the miracle cannot occur. If the possibility is missed, it waits for another day.

However, when you listen to the music of 'When I consider everything that grows . . .' and 'Should

I compare thee to a summer's day?' and then the sound of 'Brexit', it has the sound of excrement. It is sick-making.

We can be deeply touched by what only a word can evoke. And the same goes for a melody. The two come together in a special form called poetry. This will become immortal, unforgettable, when the words and their inner melody are inseparable.

Listen!

> I must go down to the seas again,
> To the lonely sea and the sky,
> And all I ask is a tall ship
> And a star to steer her by . . .

In the first line, there is a pleasant flow of sound. Then 'lonely' and 'lonely sea' cannot fail to touch our feelings.

The next line begins ' . . . And all I ask is a tall ship . . . ' Then, unexpected in the flow, comes ' . . . and a star to steer her by', and we become aware of the alliteration of 'sea' and 'sky' and 'star' and 'steer', and then the harmonious concluding rhymes of 'sky' and 'by'.

Woe to any composer who adds instruments and voices—as in so much that we call 'operatic'—he is only smothering the fine taste of the cake with rich and sugary icing.

Here we see the essential elements present in poems in any language which combine to make what we call poetry a deeply moving, haunting form of human expression.

If actors are able to live the movement with only some parts of their body, it is because so many parts are blocked. A singer listens with only the neurones that are useful—to hell with the rest.

Quarter-ear Music

From very early on my interest was in films, and I was struck by how the respected pattern that led to Oscar-winning scores was always for big orchestras, as though the composer could feel he was accompanying the story with his own symphony. The models were above all Tchaikovsky, Rachmaninov and eventually Prokofiev. The greatest word of praise for an orchestration was 'lush'.

Then, the moment of revelation. Two scores made an astonishing breakthrough. First, Carol Reed and Graham Greene's *The Third Man*, with Orson Welles in action. Here, the score was a single phrase, a handful of notes played with the clear, transparent texture of a zither. Our attention was entirely taken by the unfolding pattern of the story, and this attention was touchingly renewed each time this tiny melody returned.

Then, in a very different context, René Clément's unforgettable *Jeux interdits* (score by Narciso Yepes) brought tears to the eyes each time it penetrated into our awareness, totally taken by the story, with a Spanish guitar playing again and again a haunting phrase.

Composers for films have come to see the value of the simple phrase repeated at well-chosen moments and supported by very light, undemanding instrumentation. Two directors who understood this spring to mind. In *Barry Lyndon*, Kubrick used, often to haunting effect, melodic phrases from Schubert and Handel that touch the heart without any need to recognise their sources. On every level Kubrick was a master of cinema, and in the same way Andrei Tarkovsky, the inheritor of Eisenstein and Pudovkin, made his strange stories vibrate with a few simple notes. The one necessity was simplicity, and the common ancestor was the solo piano, playing along to the action of the silent film.

Life is In Between

ABCDEFGHI

Imagine giving a child this close-knit jumble of letters as a way of learning the alphabet. Years could go by with no result. It is in the infinitesimal gaps that life comes through. Our need in every form is to become more and more sensitive to detail. Between one letter and another, between one word and another—even at top speed—there is always a tiny gap opening on silence, on nothingness.

In *The Spirit of Noh*, the Japanese master Zeami gave a simple basic guide that has never left me. 'Jo, ha, kyu.' It is the articulation of a flow that can never halt—there can be a pause, yes, but never a complete break. Jo-ha-kyu has many images—like 'dawn, noon, twilight' or 'birth, growth, maturity'. But it is always a quality that is rising to fulfilment. What is essential is to recognise that it is about flow and is never a full stop—it is a springboard where each end is a beginning. For the performer, each gesture has a beginning, a development and an attitude which at once is the 'Jo' of the next cycle. For the Noh theatre, this demands a special quality of attention.

Bunraku, the ancient Japanese puppet theatre, offers a quite uncanny materialisation of this, where a team of hidden animators, with no way of seeing what the puppets are doing way above their heads, can feel one another's vibrations and allow complex patterns of dance or combat to materialise.

Another equally astonishing expression of this is in the Balinese drummers who, without a conductor, allow thrilling passages of ever-changing rhythms to flow between them. To bring this home to our world of music, it is all a question of listening.

I have always been drawn to the piano tuner. A piano tuner has no method, no system, but has inherited, probably from his parents and back through the generations, a simple awareness. The tuner plays a note, the strings vibrate together, and he gently presses on his hammer. Most of us would soon be satisfied, but the tuner covers the keyboard, more and more acutely aware of every fine shade of sound, only to return, never satisfied, to each note, one by one, and then ultimately a string of sounds as melody and harmony. This is a level of discernment that goes way beyond the quarter tones of Western music.

Incidental Music

us. As we have already observed, the four notes that begin Beethoven's Fifth Symphony can create a response everywhere. But the subtle force that gives life and transforms the sequence will only arise if there is this space for the unknown to appear. Often this is a link to gentleness. Too strong an affirmation can slam the door.

To return to *Musique concrète* . . .

'This will interest you,' I was told. I was taken to a drab little street in a Paris suburb. Here a broken garden gate gave onto a passage where there was a welcoming figure, Pierre Henry. 'You are interested in my music?' 'Yes,' I answered promptly. 'Come in,' he said.

His place of work was a small basement with no trace of musical instruments. For a moment, I remembered the couple who had played me their one-note composition, to be repeated across time and space. They at least had strings and a bow. Here there was nothing but a few microphones, some boards, some sheets of metal, some hammers, a couple of tape recorders and a series of consoles with reels of tape, handles, buttons, dials.

'Listen.' Pierre Henry turned a handle and the reel of tape began to play. A deafening screech filled the silence, followed by a long series of thuds. 'This,' he said, 'is my new material for today. There is no end to what I can make of it.'

Deftly manipulating the handles, he began transforming the basic sounds from crashes until, as they slowly became interesting, there were vibrations that gradually blended with one another. 'The range,' he said, 'is limitless. I can record them one on top of the other—two can become many—and then I can take tapes from a music library and my spectrum of sound becomes an orchestra that no existing orchestra could match.' I was more and more fascinated by his energy and enthusiasm.

'The first step only needs technicians. Then it is over to the composer. Just think what Stravinsky or Scriabin could have done if they had had this possibility.'

At the time, there was only Pierre Schaeffer, working for the French radio, who was exploring in this way. He had made a symphony out of a pattern of sound in a busy railway station—la Gare du Nord.

A whole new world was opening up using the possibilities given by recording and loudspeakers. Major composers like Pierre Boulez were drawn to explore 'stereoscopic' sound, as it was then called, where the placing of the speaker was an essential part of the listener's experience.

I was asked by the Royal Shakespeare Company (which was then directed by Anthony Quayle) to make a production in Stratford with Laurence Olivier and Vivien Leigh of *Titus Andronicus*—a play that had never been performed in the very place dedicated to Shakespeare as its violence was considered shameful and unworthy of their native son.

I felt that if we could create a pagan world of the fire and of the beauty that certain recent exhibitions of pagan art had revealed then the cruelty and violence could take their natural place. I could think of no composer ready to make such sound, so I decided to try myself. To make my own concrete music I had my tape recorder, my piano and a very willing and resourceful friend, Bill, who had a tiny recording studio of his own with just a bank of consoles on which sounds could be played at any speed, then edited, then re-recorded again and again. He was delighted to help. But first I needed to search for a basic sound to be treated and manipulated in the way Pierre Henry had indicated, and I found what I wanted when I stuck a microphone into the belly of my piano and stamped on the loud pedal. The entire keyboard resonated, the strings throbbed, and the woodwork of the closed instrument gave fullness to the sound. This was the basic piece of 'Concrete' that I took to Bill to explore transforming.

Out of this came the disturbing throbs, which resounded through a world of black and red columns where Vivien, as Lavinia, had her tongue and hands cut off.

For me, every form of music was an inseparable part of the whole to which every production aspires. For my first production at Stratford, *Love's Labour's Lost*, I had taken the basic imagery from the paintings of Watteau—scenes of charming, elegant young people enjoying the chatter, the food and drinks of picnics in the open air. In my head I heard some music—light and charming—that became an inseparable part of the movement of the flowing, silken costumes, the graceful moves of the actors and the final, somewhat elegant song heralding the end of summer and the coming of autumn.

Then, when I returned to Stratford to do *Romeo and Juliet*, I had already had my first experience—in Tangier—of the burning heat of the south. It pointed to the need in *Romeo and Juliet* to feel the heat of the streets that so easily led to anger and fighting. At once, fate brought me a radio version of *Don Quixote*, for which a Spanish composer had written the score. This was far from what any English composer could bring, and at once Roberto Gerhard became part of the treasure.

Two for One
and One for All

There are countless ways of understanding the word 'harmony', but in every form of music there is a basic understanding that some vibrations can come together and make one sound in which two become one.

Near to home, in Western music, we find the duet—on the opera stage or in the moment of marriage between two instruments, often piano and violin. Our emotions respond immediately to the pleasures of harmony penetrating and transforming discord. The supreme goal—as in every spiritual way—is unity. The duet can very naturally become a trio and then a quartet. It is as though human manifestations are ruled by a law of numbers. Two, three, four—the sequence in itself is harmonious. Every string quartet is an expression of the wondrous capacity of the ego willingly to give itself over to something greater than itself. In the best quartets, one thinking, one listening, carries the passage from violins to viola, viola to cello, cello to double bass, all four intertwining freely.

The instruments can change; a clarinet, an oboe, a voice, voices can all take over. But nine instruments is the limit—with the sole exception of the uncanny, lightning speed of movement, of shared thought and intention of some very ancient Eastern traditions of drumming. In every case, the secret is listening.

We never know who may be listening. During the war, posters warned us that 'careless talk costs lives', and in every totalitarian country you live with the danger of being overheard everywhere. Once, in Soviet days on a visit to Prague, I had an appointment in my hotel with a young woman interested in our work. We met in the lobby, got on well, chattered freely. Then to my astonishment she asked, 'Can I see your room?' We took the lift to my floor, and when we came into my room, she said, softly, 'Let's go into the bathroom.' I felt I was being given a fascinating lesson on how the sexual freedom of the sixties had penetrated the Iron Curtain. She took me by the hand, and as soon as we were in the bathroom she turned on the bath. This was going further and quicker than I could have imagined.

The taps made tremendous noise. She took my arm and sat me on the only chair, while she sat on the floor. 'Now,' she said, 'we can talk. Even with all their hidden gadgets, they'll never hear a word we say.'

This linked to a conclusion I was reaching. The difference between Chekhov and all his contemporaries was that he was a country doctor. While they were going to literary parties or studying in writers' classes, Chekhov would devotedly respond to every call, day or night, to visit patients in their home. He never had a consulting room, and as a result, day after day, he heard and observed every aspect of rural family life.

In the same way, the advantage Irish writers had over their English colleagues was that their 'school', their source of knowledge of what makes humans tick, was in the pubs, whether in Dublin or in the villages. Or, as one playwright said, it was lying on the floor in his lodgings, listening to the ever-changing voices that came up through the floorboards. It is clear that Shakespeare's knowledge of the world, of the differences between every form called men and women, came not from scholars, nor from poring over ancient texts. It came from the time he spent in the taverns and the streets. The key was quite simply—listening.

At the time when artists everywhere were questioning all the elements they had learnt to be inseparable from the form, a great creator in the world of ballet, Merce Cunningham, made with his supple, sensitive group of dancers a silent ballet. Perhaps the experiment had no future, but it had the magical effect of making us, the audience, more finely tuned to one another. It was truly unforgettable. It was the Zen of dancing.

With the same spirit of adventure, a young French dancer and choreographer, Jean Babilée, joined Roland Petit and Janine Charrat's company, Les Ballets des Champs Elysées. Petit had invited a fashionable Parisian figure, the poet, painter and film maker, Jean Cocteau, to devise a ballet for his company—and for Babilée.

Cocteau wrote a little scenario, *Le Jeune Homme et la Mort*. A young man in a garret, Jean Babilée, was tying a rope to a beam and preparing to hang himself. When he would fall lifeless to the floor, the designer, my friend Georges Wakhevitch, had arranged for the whole attic to be lifted into the flies revealing the rooftops of Paris, with a winking neon sign in the distance, while Nathalie Philippart, as Death, would come to lead him away across the roofs.

To give the dancers the support they were accustomed to, Cocteau and Petit devised a complex pattern of rhythms. For every rehearsal, there was the same little percussion group (live or recorded) that gave them structure and the breath of silence between the beats. When it came to the first performance at the Théâtre des Champs Elysées, there was a surprise waiting for them. The percussion group had gone, and in its place a small orchestra played Bach. They were at once lifted to a new level, and the theme—Youth and Death—was in us all.

PART TWO

The Speed of Thought

Music—as Shakespeare said—is the food of love and must be treated lovingly.

But young readers beware! This is not a method, nor is it a conclusion. No!

Play! We play jazz, we play allegro, we play andante, we play *marche funèbre*, we play a farce, we play Oedipus, and for the parts of the body it is with equal joy. Even the instrument responds better when the muscles are lightened by joy. Preparation at first needs hard work, we clamber up the hill, then we jump on our sledge and are carried away.

I had staged many plays that made a strong impact on Broadway—*Marat/Sade, The Visit* and *Irma la Douce*. A young ambitious producer, Saint Subber, contacted me to create a musical based on *House of Flowers*. Terrifying because on the one hand it drew the finest talents in storytelling, lyric writing, melody making, singing, dancing, choreography, staging, lighting—there was no end—all demanding the highest quality with a free, creative imagination. An El Dorado. But the other side of the picture was the terrifying pressure. I met a young director on the opening night of the first important show he had been given to direct. He tried unsuccessfully to hide his nerves. In a few hours, his future would be settled. A hit and all would be well. But a flop . . . He would no longer be able to pay his rent, he would lose his girlfriend and with her all the dreams they had built together. I saw the two sides of the American dream, and it all came down to cash. Karl Marx sat for months in the British Museum library studying, analysing, pondering before sending out the first great cry of alarm. This led Brecht to try, in play after play, to warn the ignorant of the dangers that surround them in a world dominated by a blood-drenched word, 'Capitalism'.

No Businesss Like
Show Business

The Old and the New

'Broadway' and 'Hollywood' have long been words of derision. So I take a secret pleasure in telling people who speak movingly of the impact on them of the *Midsummer Night's Dream* that I put on in Stratford, London and New York in the early seventies that the great influence that made this possible was my experience on Broadway.

Every year back then I would find a reason to go to New York. By contrast with the stately, unchanging, middle-class London theatre, Broadway was vibrating with new people, new ways, new life. Of course, the often ruthless aim was success: great notices on the opening night or else the show had no chance of survival. But in exchange, all the very best talent flocked to Broadway. And it wasn't all musicals; the straight theatre too had the top adventurous new talents—Arthur Miller, Tennessee Williams, Edward Albee—and ground-breaking directors like Elia Kazan.

But the great magnet in New York was indeed the musical. After years of being a cosy entertainment for tired businessmen and their wives, came *Oklahoma!*, *South Pacific*, and on to the unforgettable shocks of, on one level, *West Side Story* and on the other *Guys and*

Dolls! Here, the Shakespeare model was incarnate: never to lose the common touch. So a hit could travel round the world and become a household name.

For myself, there were two experiences inseparable from Broadway. One was the first visit of the Chinese acrobats. They demonstrated that the way to suggest the fairies of the spirit world was not with pretty, transparent costumes on girlish dancers. It was by evoking lightness with the lightness of seemingly effortless acrobatics. The other eye-opener came from Jerome Robbins. The musical called on top choreographers to bring a new life to the customary routines of the operetta, to develop their own dancers in their own way. Robbins was already one of the luminaries of the New York City Ballet. His new work was called *Dances at a Gathering*. A small group of dancers are discovered round a piano. The pianist began to play the first notes, notes that belonged to the ballet world—Chopin. The dancers were all dressed in simple, white, everyday clothes. Gone were the moonlight, the painted trees, the tutus. Instead, gradually as though responding for the first time to the notes, they left the piano, and, in an unchanging bright light, there flowed a series of *pas de deux* for man and girl, easing into wider animation when the whole ensemble left the piano to make patterns of light movement.

When we needed to find a path to the hidden life of *A Midsummer Night's Dream*, my constant collaborators, the composer Richard Peaslee and the designer Sally Jacobs, had long been fed our own experiences in our workshops, but what Broadway gave us was the need and the courage to develop what we had begun to discover.

House of Flowers

In New York, our anxious young producer could sleep quietly as we assembled a foolproof team.

Truman Capote, a young, gay writer whose books were on every coffee table, had proposed turning his own short story *House of Flowers* into a musical. He would write the script and the lyrics for a top composer, Harold Arlen, famous amongst other hits for Judy Garland's 'Over the Rainbow'. Also joining the team was no less than George Balanchine, the purest of choreographers. And our star was the most vibrant Broadway actress, singer Pearl Bailey. Yes, he could sleep happily. It could not go wrong. But it did. How could such a seeming hit become a flop? I began painfully to discover the unknown rules of Broadway.

In all my London experiences, the director was the top dog. He had the final say on how his show should be made; all the elements—cast, music, settings—were his territory. In the London theatre jargon of the time the director was called the producer. ('Director' was a business term referring to the Managing Director of a company.) Of course, above the producer was the management, who usually owned or had long-term deals with the theatres. Naturally, the producer would listen to their comments and happily accept good advice from experienced eyes with a certain detachment. New York was a very different scene. The person called the producer had become the absolute boss. He was the management, and he found and provided the cash. By contrast, the person called the director could, like all the team, be hired and fired at the producer's whim. Before opening on Broadway, a show would often go for an out-of-town try-out—a valuable system allowing changes to be made but which was also a ruthless process whereby, overnight, writers, actors, directors could be sent packing. On my very first trip to New York I was the guest of a top producer who was interested in a show we were doing in London. He kindly offered to get me a ticket for the musical that everyone was talking about. I was very disappointed by it, and when I saw him the next day I began to give him my criticisms. He cut me off sharply. 'Nonsense!' he said, 'It's the hottest seat in town!'

I gradually learned the tremendous advantage of creating a play in the secure conditions of the London West End, and if it happened to click, it would be that very production which enterprising producers would invite to New York. With *House of Flowers* I learnt that the American musical had a complex series of rules, unknown to the visiting director. Truman Capote had never written a musical, so it was the responsibility of the director to coach him, rewrite after rewrite, until his script conformed to what Broadway musicals demanded. Step by step, composer, choreographer, designer knew that they too had to conform to what was demanded of them by the all-knowing eye of the man who paid—the producer.

Harold Arlen and Truman Capote's first attempts at lyric writing were far from what an audience had been conditioned to expect. Marlene Dietrich was such a friend and fan of Harold Arlen that she moved in to encourage and guide him through a show-business world that she knew only too well.

Pearl Bailey was a long-established singing star—and was in no way convinced by the other unformed but talented singers in the cast, mostly recruited from the West Indies. I saw the unbridgeable distance between these two worlds in rehearsal when she came to me to pour out her anger against a young singer who dared to take herself too seriously: 'Who does she think she is? She carries on as though she's a star. I tried to slap her down, to get some sense into her. So I said to her, "You think you're a star? Just listen to me, honey! If you're a star, just tell me—where are your furs, where are your diamonds, where are your cars?"'

And as we rehearsed, our poor young producer, watching me at work, did not feel he had the authority to step in and say to me, 'No! You're getting it wrong.' He just sat and suffered. And of course in Broadway terms the show could not come together.

The story was a good one. The House of Flowers was a brothel in the port of a Caribbean island. A group of enchanting ladies were the Flowers. At the rise of the curtain they were sitting sadly hoping for a ship to bring some customers. Harold Arlen had given them an enchanting chorus that began 'Waiting. Waiting. Waiting, it is so irritating. Waiting for a ship to come by.' Then the story started with cockfights and voodoo. By the time the show had—very rapidly—given up the ghost, I had already left for Europe, but my greatest disappointment was that the score was so quickly forgotten. For years, in Paris, I hoped to make a musical free of Broadway pressures. However, I had already been deeply immersed in the world of musicals in the free atmosphere of London at the time.

Popular music is always a guide. When the great American musicals swept across the world, neither London nor Paris had anything to compare, and we realised how poor our old-fashioned forms of musical theatre had become. A new young generation began to explore what could be alive for them then. Deep in the world of rock, they were to make musicals that did not copy American models.

Irma la Douce

Meanwhile in Paris, the long tradition established by operetta had led to Maurice Chevalier, Arletty, Piaf—each opening a popular and accessible world of their own. But the cosy operetta form persisted, until one day in a tiny space—Le Théâtre Gramont—a certain journalist called Alexandre Breffort found the discarded manuscript of a play that he had written, and which the boulevard theatres had refused to put on, about a tart with a heart of gold. It was called *Irma la Douce*. The Théâtre de Gramont was prepared to take a risk as it had a tiny cast, it was scenically simple and orchestrally very minimal, and Marguerite Monnot, composer of much of Edith Piaf's repertoire, had agreed to write the score! On a very small scale it was an immediate hit. I went to see it with my two friends, Julian More, whose own musical comedy, *Grab Me a Gondola*, was opening the same year, and Monty Norman, a jazz singer who went on to compose the original James Bond theme. It was obvious to all three of us that we must find a way of bringing *Irma la Douce* to London.

We looked everywhere for a young singer/actress to play Irma, marvellously given in Paris by the popular singer Colette Renard. We found Elizabeth Seal, who eventually took the show with her and us to New York with a ruthless and dynamic producer, David Merrick. From the start, the lightness, the direct appeal of the music, which could touch young and old alike, made this a true hit in the line of the new musicals.

The Beggar's Opera

an intrinsic part of the role, not with a rough streetwise voice, but with a voice that could astonish music lovers. So he began to train with a top-level opera voice teacher. The result was that, on every level, style and elegance became uncomfortable bedfellows with the rough world of the beggars. Gradually, each scene became a battlefield between the two of us.

In the end, the film was not the rough work I had looked for nor the exquisite gem that both Olivier and Wilcox dreamed of. Our film was a non-starter, a 'distinguished' flop. Its expensive elegance no longer suited our time. Brecht and Kurt Weill had restored the balance with their *Threepenny Opera* in 1928. Their total commitment to militant communism made the beggar's tale perfect material for a timely masterpiece. The power of Kurt Weill's music led to the ultimate irony: 'Mack the Knife' became a worldwide hit like 'Lilli Marlene'. The tune penetrated the iron gates and the high walls of Buckingham Palace. The Queen knew nothing of *The Beggar's Opera* nor *The Threepenny Opera*. She only knew she loved the tune of 'Mack the Knife', which was in three-four waltz time. So when she opened a palace ball for the cream of London society and all the Diplomatic Corps, she would take Prince Philip by the hand, lead him on to the dance floor and open the ball with . . . 'Mack the Knife'.

However, the battle that had been our *Beggar's Opera* was followed by a happy post-war period. Larry's enchanting wife, Vivien Leigh, did everything to bring us together. Nourished by weekends in their country manor, a good friendship grew between the four of us—Larry, Vivien, my wife Natasha and me. When I was asked by the new director of Stratford's Memorial Theatre which play of Shakespeare I would like to stage, this was when I suggested *Titus Andronicus*, which, as I mentioned before, had never been staged there because of its violence.

The Oliviers were already playing at Stratford, and both accepted readily to be part of this adventure. I came to the first rehearsal ready for another battle, only to find the doors fly open and a welcoming Larry and Vivien ready and waiting. The work with Larry and Vivien unrolled in happy harmony, and the result was a work we could take round Europe in joyful partnership.

Words and Music

In the rehearsals of *The Tragedy of Carmen*, I would ask the singers first to speak the words, then, in a close relationship with the partner in the scene, look into their eyes and speak the words, so gently that the melody, already present in the words, could arise by itself. I would ask the singers to leave aside all snobbism in relation to grand opera as opposed to musical comedies and allow themselves to sing many Broadway hits, then songs by singers such as Leonard Cohen, Marlene Dietrich and Edith Piaf. They would at once see that words, melody and tempo are one. But the motor—the inspiration—comes from the words. When Bizet read Mérimée's short story about Carmen, when Tchaikovsky first heard Pushkin's *Eugene Onegin* or *Queen of Spades*, it was an immediate sense of character and situation that touched them and made melodies arise in them.

When Jonathan Miller filmed a rehearsal of *La Bohème* that he had directed, there was, naturally, only the rehearsal pianist and his piano, and naturally there was no need for any singer to project. As a result, the whole tale of Mimi and the Bohemian comrades became deeply moving. I have always especially loved *Bohème* and wished to direct it. I have seen so many productions, often of top quality, but the experience of the opera in rehearsal was the most touching one of all. Food for thought.

Don Giovanni

Tradition had always told us that *Don Giovanni* was a story with a moral; the Don was a ruthless egoist, bent on his own satisfaction but possessed of great charm—so much a prisoner of his sexual urges that he left not only broken hearts but even corpses in his wake. So while we could laugh and relish his many conquests and adventures, the end of the story showed the hell he so rightly deserved. Such a reading of the work seemed to me in contradiction with the music itself. I began to feel that Mozart both loved and identified himself with the lover.

Somewhere, the melodies were Mozart himself. To suit the demands of the time, the libretto had to end with the damnation of the seducer and a chorus of rejoicing that the sinner had paid for his sins. I could not bring myself to feel that Mozart's music was there to give a conveniently moral end to the work.

Mozart has been a fertile ground for long periods of misunderstandings. The Viennese school—a world of rich cream and pastries—saw Mozart as an elegant little charmer. So the aim of performers was to give lace-edged elegance to music that only gradually reasserted the power and passion of the young composer.

In the same way, Mozart's own turbulent sexuality was glossed over. As I plunged more and more deeply into *Don Giovanni*, the clearer it became that, just like Shakespeare, Mozart could not—and would not—judge and condemn his characters according to the conventional morality of the time. As I worked with a deeply true acting and singing talent, Peter Mattei, we discovered that Mozart clearly loved his Don. We improvised in our Parisian base, the Théâtre des Bouffes du Nord—far from the associations of an opera house. We had two casts. These two casts worked together and exchanged roles—two casts as one—learning from one another on the way, and gradually came to reject the conventional ending, where the Don reaps his true deserts in Hell while the virtuous burghers rejoice in conventional choruses. To us, the really touching music came from the seduced women, in no way revengeful, but truly reliving this rewarding moment in their lives. Out of this came the simple scenic invention of having the Don returning from the other world and listening with compassion to the women he had loved and who had loved him in return. As in *The Magic Flute*, it was love that only music can express.

A Magic Flute

As so often, it was my regular collaborator Marie-Hélène Estienne who brought me the right person at the right time. The composer and pianist Franck Krawczyk had played with a vocal ensemble at the Bouffes du Nord, and Marie-Hélène had been fascinated by the freedom and sensitivity he brought with him. He at once responded to the proposition to reconsider—even rediscover—*The Magic Flute* with us. With no preconceptions, we spent a part of the summer exploring the score with Franck at the keyboard. It became clear that, after *Carmen* and *Pelléas*, the Bouffes was the ideal place for this work to return to its playful intimacy. It arose very naturally, calling to be re-explored. It seemed clear that Mozart's inner world, along with the exquisite delicacy of its lightness and humour, brought into sharp relief the burden that this work had carried for so long, thanks to the complicated devices and decorations that directors and designers had imposed on it. Even the music was often weighed down by too-large orchestras in too-large amphitheatres, forcing the singers to sing and act in a style that grand opera expects. Franck lovingly arranged the score for a piano with the knowledge that a fine grand piano is an orchestra in itself, and it was obvious to us all that his fingers on his piano were all the orchestra we needed.

After our usual, prolonged period of trial and error, it became clear and essential that Franck needed to be present not only at each rehearsal but also in performance. With the piano close to the singers, the work could live and sing in a fresh way.

We called it _A Magic Flute_ in the way we called our _Pelléas: Impressions of Pelléas_, so as not to claim for a moment that we were proposing a definitive new version. It was in this way that it went on its journey—as far as New York, where to our surprise and relief it was accepted and welcomed by the very conservative and dominant critics there. This is not the place to go into more detail of the _Flute_ adventures, but this has enabled me to record how Franck became an irreplaceable part of our musical journey.

The Prisoner

Many years went by until we picked up a theme that refused to let us go, *The Prisoner*. A legend that came from a true situation I experienced many years earlier in Afghanistan. With Marie-Hélène we began to build our team of collaborators, and it was obvious that the first place would go to Franck. He had been with us on *The Suit*, where he had attended every rehearsal at his piano, proposing unexpected pieces of Schubert that surprisingly seemed made to partake in this tale.

For *The Prisoner*, Franck sat with an electric keyboard, listening and improvising. Day after day, haunting fragments of melody arose from his own creative imagination. Gradually, with the actors, a form began to appear. Then the day came when Franck said, very simply: 'Nothing of what I propose is right. The sound that goes most truly with this piece is silence.' And wherever we play *The Prisoner*, audiences are deeply touched by the many moments of silence that have become an inseparable part of the story.

Labour of Love

Very young, reading *War and Peace* for the first time, I was touched by the music of the name Natasha. I knew at once that this was the companion destiny had prepared for me. When, in real life, we first set eyes on one another, Natasha Parry was just sixteen. Everything grew from this moment.

Later, it was the very special, fine sensitivity that shone through her beauty which touched all those she met. She very early caught the eye of casting directors and began a career in films, then in theatre.

But, for the hurly-burly, rough and tumble of show business, her qualities were too special. I began to feel that she needed to be guided to the roles she could illuminate in her own way. I felt that this was my responsibility and together we worked on Beckett's *Oh les beaux jours* (*Happy Days*)—a radiant and demanding monologue which Beckett had written for the wondrous French actress Madeleine Renaud.

We played in Paris at the Bouffes du Nord, but it was a hard task for Natasha to overcome the memories of Madeleine. Nevertheless the part quickly became her own, and the production travelled the world with a quality appreciated everywhere—even on a short visit in London. England was the ultimate challenge, as Beckett had written the play with equal care in both languages. But we continued to perform in French, because the English version, *Happy Days*, had a very different flavour. One could always feel the presence of Beckett's master, James Joyce, and of Dublin. In English, the play naturally belonged to the rough, down-to-earth texture of a theatre transformed by the gritty reality of *Look Back in Anger*.

But our French version called for a very different quality, one that needed lightness and presence. No one was better suited to this, even in France, than Natasha.

In London we played not in the West End but in the Riverside Studios in West London, where it was very well received. Everything pointed to our returning to play this version for a run in the West End. I did everything to resist this, as I was convinced that the powerful tradition of the English Beckett would make for a useless rivalry.

Natasha brought his same clarity to Shakespeare, playing Cordelia in a television version of *King Lear* with Orson Welles.

Naturally, I began to wonder what Shakespeare role she could tackle without entering into the ruthless rivalry and competition that these parts attract. Together, we began to listen to the Sonnets and discovered that they were not just isolated poems. They are part of a story. In all the plays, we have no right to say, 'That's Shakespeare's point of view', as he always, with every word, allowed his characters to speak for themselves. But the Sonnets are like Shakespeare's private diary. He notes down all his impressions on love entirely from his own personal experience—with many dark and fair ladies and equally with beautiful young men. We discovered that the Sonnets contain the first meetings, the springtime of love, the comfortable middle period and then the cruel, painful, suspiciousness leading to jealousy, recriminations, separations and rarely reconciliations. We called our project, in Shakespeare's own words, *Love is My Sin*.

We found an ideal partner in Bruce Myers (and later, Michael Pennington), and evolved a form which began with Natasha's 'When I consider every thing that grows . . .' leading on through all that every lover knows 'Like as the waves . . .'

Music was needed to bind the parts into a whole, so I asked our dear collaborator Franck Krawczyk to join us. He was so sensitive to the music of the words that he could find the themes and melody that were always perfectly in tune, only discovering the meaning of the English words gradually though the long tour. With *Love is My Sin*, I wished at all costs to avoid the cliché of Elizabethan music—which luckily Franck did not know. Feeling a natural kinship with Shakespeare's language, Franck drew on Couperin: Couperin father, he insisted, not Couperin son.

It was clear as we began to perform that there was indeed a story, a love story, leading from the joys of a relationship being born and shared.

Natasha's very special qualities were in her beautiful and touching sensitivity. These enabled her to bring a new vision to plays that seemed to be well known—as in *The Cherry Orchard*. She brought audiences to the heart of Chekhov which they had thought they knew; and it was a revelation. Jean-Claude Carrière made this new version hand in hand with Natasha's mother, Elisaveta Lavrova.

This very naturally prepared the way, many years later, for the deeply moving *Ta Main dans la mienne—Your Hand in Mine*—based on correspondence between Chekhov and his wife, Olga Knipper. Gaev from our *Cherry Orchard*, Michel Piccoli, played Chekhov; Natasha, of course, was Knipper.

The Sound of Silence

Very early in the work of our International Centre for Theatre Research based at the Bouffes, as we explored sounds and languages, we became more aware that the deaf possess a highly developed language of their own, inseparable from movements of the hands and above all the fingers. For an actor to explore and develop all his instruments, this field of study seemed essential.

In Paris we visited a school, founded by the Abbé Pierre, who had first introduced sign language to France. We became aware of how slow our usual language is when we saw the deaf using a language much closer to the speed of thought.

This speed is there to different degrees in the fingers of every instrumentalist, in the total body presence linking arms, hands, fingers, eyes in every conductor. It seems to be the fruit of practice and effort, but what we are seeing is the manifestation of an unknown source which can infuse and illuminate every cell and fibre in sometimes very young prodigies.

In America, there was a young company called the National Theatre of the Deaf, run by David Hays. We invited them to work with us in Paris—a very rewarding experience for us all. We discovered how sensitive they were to rhythm, the only sound that could reach up and penetrate into them through the soles of their feet when the rhythms made the floor vibrate—vibration, the pulse of the silent world.

Once, in Barcelona, I was taken to visit the great singer and dancer of flamenco, Pastora Imperio. She was very old and could no longer rise to greet a visitor; she just gave me a tiny smile. My friend introduced me, then spoke glowingly of all his memories of her art. She nodded, sat motionless. Then her lips moved. My friend bent over her. 'She's speaking in Catalan . . . She says she would be happy to sing and dance for you.' Of course we knew she couldn't move, but she felt that this was what we expected of her, and we sat hoping that at least she could feel our respectful attention. Then, impulses began to bring tiny tremors into her fingers. Gradually, her whole hand became alive. And then an almost invisible movement of her lips, her mouth, her eyes. Time ceased. Bit by bit, those minute possibilities became the vehicle of her inner passion. We were spellbound. When the time came for her to indicate that she had poured out her heart for us and the end was reached, we knew we had been uniquely privileged. We had seen the great Pastora Imperio with all the joy and tragedy of her art. There were tears in our eyes as we rose and murmured 'Adios!'

A friend for many years in South Africa was the black actor John Kani. At the time, the pitiless rules of Apartheid forbade any black actor to show himself on a stage in front of a white audience. John and the white theatre director Barney Simon were searching for ways to bypass this taboo. Then they realised that in a market, for instance, commerce must be the only criterion. A market could not survive, nor even exist, if laws prevented customers of every colour spending their money on food and objects, collected and sold by an unselected mixture of coloured skins. So, why not a theatre, they thought: a mixture of entertainers telling stories to an equally mixed audience. And so the Market Theatre in Johannesburg was born. And it went from strength to strength, joined by a highly talented and deeply committed white writer, Athol Fugard. They only ran into trouble when the Royal Court Theatre in London invited Athol and his two actors, Winston Ntshona and John Kani, to play *The Island*, Athol's hard-hitting play about life in the dreaded open-air prison under the burning sun, Robben Island. The South African police tried to prevent this by forbidding to grant exit visas to the two actors. But—such was the astonishing stupidity of dictatorships—the production was able to go ahead when Athol Fugard agreed to accompany his actors to London, which a white man was entitled to do provided he declared them as his valet and his gardener. The impact of the play in London was extraordinary.

Some years later, the rules weakened, so, with our first little group, we could visit the Market ourselves. We set up a series of workshops, open equally to black and white young actors. I proposed an exercise we had developed that we called the Tightrope! This was later filmed by my son Simon. In it, the actor applies his imagination to every part of his body as he tries to bring reality to the task of crossing a circle on an imaginary tightrope. After the young Africans had tried, discovering literally all the pitfalls, I asked John Kani to take part. A moment of hesitation. Would he reveal himself—a revered figure in front of a young group of students? I knew he had great pain in his legs and could no longer move freely, but to my surprise he instantly agreed. He remained seated on his chair, while all our attention went to his hands. None of us had ever seen the Tightrope so vividly brought to life, detail by detail, as John Kani, still seated, took us into the air to perform dangerous acrobatics on a thin rope, high in the air, just with his fingers.

Everything ties together. Very recently I heard of prisoners in France in a formidable jail who taught one another sign language. There was a women's block from which they were separated by a wall of spikes and barbed wire. Because they were breaking no rules, they could relieve their long confinement by teaching the women the sign language and then communicating and eventually flirting with the female prisoners, their fingers responding to necessity.

Keep Silence

There is a temple in Japan where the courtyard is a very famous stone garden. Only a great Zen master could create an ultimate empty space where, on sand finely raked and sifted every morning at dawn, there are only three small stones. The perfection of art is in the placing. In the Zen garden it would be enough to move one of the three stones a fraction of a millimetre out of its place and the living soundless music would be lost. Luckily, in Japan, no one would dare.

This famous treasure attracts an endless flow of visitors. They come to taste the presence of a living silence. Before entering there is a large sign asking them to 'Keep Silence'—this is not a grammatical mistake but a request. Here, we are invited together to preserve something very precious—pure silence. And in this way be responsible for a national treasure.

Near San Francisco, there are ancient woods where the tall trees reaching to the sky are pillars that go way beyond the creation of the finest cathedral buildings. There they were worked in stone, but here it is the living texture of trees that create the purest of silence. It is only at dawn today that this vibrant silence can be experienced.

Poets seek to capture this magic, but words cannot go as far as music. Sometimes, as in lieder, the marriage between note and phrase can be felt, and the greatest music again calls on us all to listen. Between the notes, silence appears; then with love and respect we all keep silence. For a moment, the listening brings the precise quality of being loved, honoured and protected.

Once, in the Sahara, I climbed up a dune and, looking down, saw that the hollow in front of me was very deep. I slithered down the sandy wall, and when I reached the bottom I was completely isolated from the desert, and all its tiny sounds had vanished. There, for the first time, I actually experienced the living presence of total silence.

When, long after, a friend returning from an arduous climb in the mountains said, 'In this clear air, full of light, Silence was so alive I felt I could touch it', I knew what he meant.

A truly remarkable man I knew, William Segal, was a perfect host to his friends and would constantly invite them to intimate dinners with dishes carefully prepared by his loving wife, Marielle, and the finest of wines carefully tested on the sensitive palate of the host himself. In his very last days, knowing the end was in sight, he would not allow himself to forego his hospitality to his most intimate friends. He would fill their glasses then take up his own empty glass, and in order to maintain his gentle ritual of toasts he would murmur, so none of us could feel abandoned, 'I drink the silence.'

A touching old English saying arises in my mind: 'Words fail me.' So this is the moment to end. The most precious thing is: 'Keep Silence.'

Peter Brook

Peter Brook is one of the world's best-known theatre directors. Outstanding in a career full of remarkable achievements are his productions of *Titus Andronicus* (1955) with Laurence Olivier, *King Lear* (1962) with Paul Scofield, and *The Marat/Sade* (1964) and *A Midsummer Night's Dream* (1970), both for the Royal Shakespeare Company. Since moving to Paris and establishing the International Centre for Theatre Research in 1970 and the International Centre for Theatre Creation when he opened the Théâtre des Bouffes du Nord in 1974, he has produced a series of events which push at the boundaries of theatre, such as *The Conference of the Birds* (1976), *The Ik* (1975), *The Mahabharata* (1985) and *The Tragedy of Carmen* (1981) to name but a few. His films include *Lord of the Flies* (1963), *King Lear* (1970), *The Mahabharata* (1989), *Tell Me Lies* (restored 2013) and *Meetings with Remarkable Men* (restored 2017). His hugely influential books, from *The Empty Space* (1968) to *Tip of the Tongue* (2017), have been published in many languages throughout the world.